by
GERALD McDERMOTT

Sun Flight

FOUR WINDS PRESS
NEW YORK

LIBRARY OF CONGRESS CATALOGING IN PUBLICATION DATA

McDermott, Gerald.
    Sun flight.
    Summary: Daedalus fashions wings for the escape of himself and
his son Icarus from the Labyrinth of King Minos of Crete, but Icarus
fails to heed his father's warnings about their use.
    1. Daedalus—Juvenile literature.   2. Icarus—Juvenile litera-
ture.   [1. Daedalus.   2. Icarus.   3. Mythology, Greek]   I. Title.
PZ8.1.M159Su   398.2 [E]   79-5067
ISBN 0-590-07632-9

Published by Four Winds Press
A division of Scholastic Magazines, Inc., New York, N.Y.
Copyright © 1980 by Gerald McDermott
All rights reserved
Printed in the United States of America
Library of Congress Catalog Card Number: 79-5067
1   2   3   4   83   82   81   80

The sun glistened on the bright isle and dolphins sang in the blue Aegean sea. Daedalus, the master craftsman, surveyed his marvelous handiwork. With his son, Icarus, he had toiled for seven years on the island of Crete. He had created a palace and many wondrous things for Minos, the King.

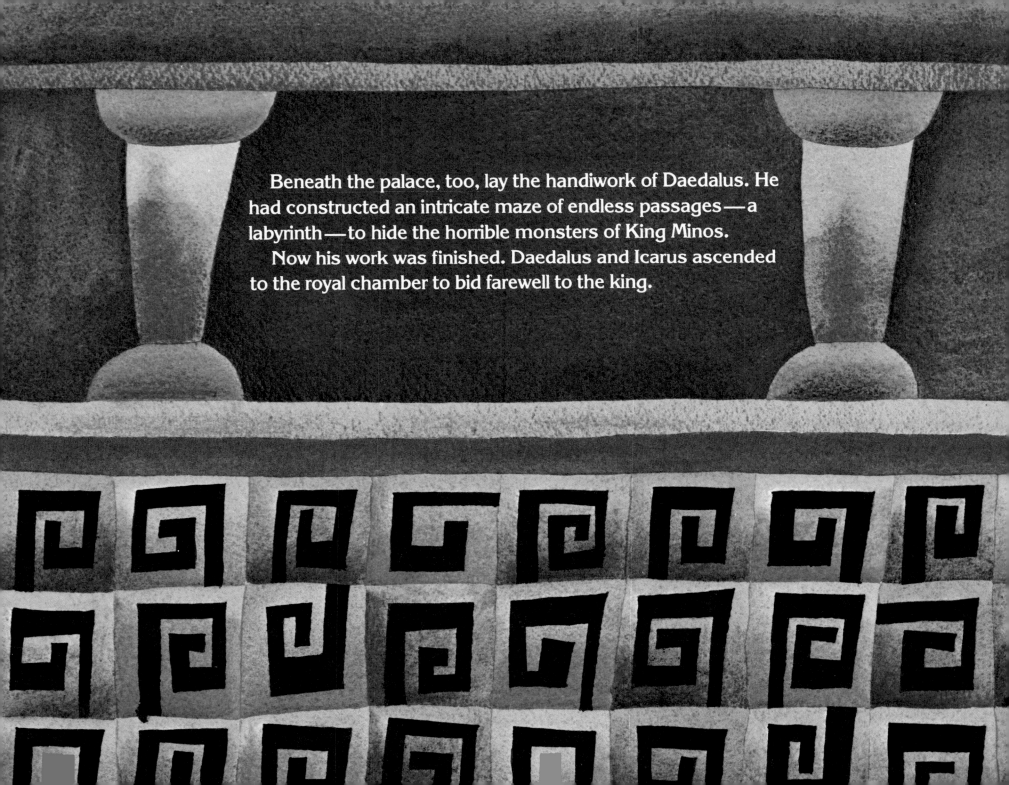

Beneath the palace, too, lay the handiwork of Daedalus. He had constructed an intricate maze of endless passages—a labyrinth—to hide the horrible monsters of King Minos.

Now his work was finished. Daedalus and Icarus ascended to the royal chamber to bid farewell to the king.

The king was angry and filled with wrath. He refused to release the artisan and his son.

"You alone know the secret of the Labyrinth!" Minos roared. "You shall not leave. I will cast you into the prison of your own making."

Minos hurled the pair into the darkness of the Labyrinth. The door was sealed. The craftsman and his son were hopelessly trapped.

Ancient ghosts floated out of the blackness to haunt them. Ancient monsters leapt up to terrify them.

Daedalus and Icarus ran blindly down the dark passages, seeking escape. Every path led to a trap, every tunnel ended in disappointment.

The imprisoned pair trembled in the cold darkness and despaired of escaping.

Then the moonlight crept into the recesses of their prison. Daedalus and his son watched as birds rose up on feathered wings, up through the dark vaults into the night sky.

Daedalus quickly set to work. He instructed Icarus to gather together the fallen feathers and then he toiled through the night. Skillfully he mounted the feathers with wax and constructed two magnificent pairs of wings.

When dawn came, Daedalus and Icarus rose up on the feathered wings. They rose up through the vaults of the Labyrinth and burst joyously into the freedom of the sky.

Daedalus cautioned Icarus.

"Fly not too low, my son, lest you fall into the cold depths of the sea.

"Fly not too high, my son, lest you perish in the burning rays of the sun.

"Fly not too fast, my son, lest your fragile wings fail you."

"Icarus…   Icarus!"

The sun glistened on the bright isle and the dolphins sang in the blue Aegean sea. But Daedalus, the master craftsman, wept bitter tears.

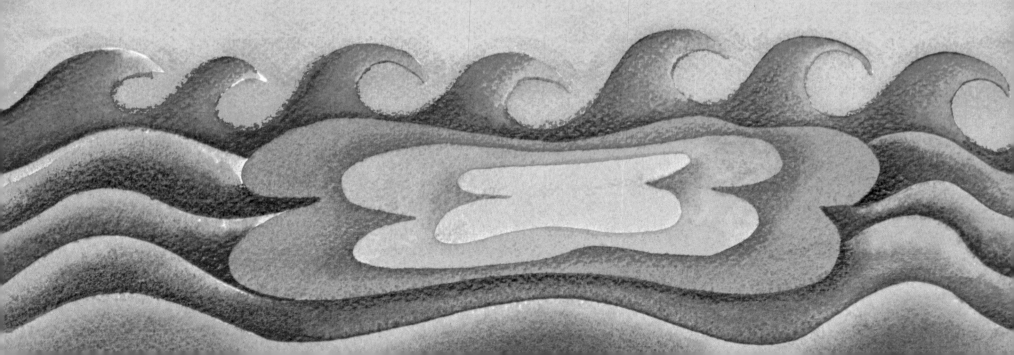